HOW TO TURN YOUR TALENT INTO A BUSINESS WORKBOOK

Easy steps to turning your talents into profit

TAUGHT BY
JANET GREEN

YES, you have what it takes to start your own business!
Let's birth it together and remember…
with GOD, ALL things are possible!

2011 © Olmstead Publishing
How to Turn Your Talent Into a Business Workbook
By Janet Green
howto@janetbusiness.com
www.janetbusiness.com

God Did It!

Front Cover Sketch by Therisiah Ngang

Cover and Formatting by Dr Phyllis M Olmstead

Olmstead Publishing
Personalized, On Demand, Small Order Publishing
www.OlmsteadPublishing.com Apopka@USA.com

Table of Contents

Author

Janet Green worked over twenty years in the hospitality industry. She started her career at a five star hotel in New York City as a PBX operator. After working six months, she was promoted to PBX supervisor, where she supervised 32 operators.

Even though she was the youngest staff member and had the fewest years of experience in her department, Janet did not let all the negative and spiteful words from her coworkers kill her enthusiasm. Instead, she used it as fuel to keep her fire burning. After only three months in that position, she was able to gain the respect and loyalty of her staff. Three years later, the company promoted her to front office supervisor.

Janet became bored in this position so she decided to transfer to the accounting department where she received numerous awards, including Associate of the Year Award. As if this did not keep her busy enough, she took on some of the human resources department responsibilities, such as planning the annual associate picnic and holiday party for their four hundred-plus associates.

Janet's general manager saw great potential in her as a director of human resources (HR) and encouraged her to start a career in the field. She transferred to HR where she spent the next two years learning all the disciplines (recruiting, employee relations, employee benefits, and payroll) in that field. She then transferred to another state as an HR Manager and one year later, she became Director of Human Resources.

As a dedicated professional, she managed to maintain high associate satisfaction ratings, reducing the amount of associates leaving the company as she maximized and promoted talented associates around her. Her love for her associates went beyond her call of duty as she supported their family successes and grieved with them during their times of distress.

As busy as she was as a Director of Human Resources, Janet consistently exemplified the importance of giving back to the community. In one year, she was able to accomplish the following:

- Fed 1,767 homeless men and children
- Collected over 100 cellular phones for the "Secure A Call Foundation"
- Collected over 65 pairs of used eye glasses for donations
- Collected over 112 pairs of used sneakers to refurbish tennis courts
- Raised funds for the "Children's Miracle Network"
- Planned and executed a hotel market picnic for over 3,000 associates and families

In July of 2009, Janet experienced the worst year of her professional career. At that time, she began to strengthen her relationship with God through prayer.

One day she prayed and asked God to close all doors that needed to be closed and to open all the doors that needed to be opened in her life. Fewer than 48 hours later, Janet noticed what she described as "all hell breaking loose" around her. First, her career as Director of Human Resources ended abruptly and 24 hours after that, her fiancé called to end their three-year relationship.

Janet then turned to God for answers as to why it seemed that everything was going wrong in her life, and then she remembered how good God is and immediately began to thank Him for her life and the lives of her sons. On the third night of this turn-of-events, God told Janet in a dream, "'You prayed for me to close all doors that needed to be closed and to open all doors that needed to be opened' and I answered your prayer." From that day forth, Janet was at peace with the things that were happening in her life.

Janet then decided it was time for her to start her own business. Even though it was no secret in her family that she was a gifted cook and had the wits of a tough business woman, they were disappointed that she would no longer do what she did best, which was taking care of others and defending the voiceless as a director of human resources.

In July of 2009, Janet started her own company, Jamaican Global Throw Down Catering Services. She started with the concept of catering for weddings, parties, and reunions. As she researched the food industry and catering business market, she realized that there were endless possibilities for her services and products. During her first year in business, she volunteered her time cooking at least once a month for charitable organizations. She now models the motto "Anyone that eats is my customer." Janet also became a member of several chambers of commerce in the local Orlando, Florida area.

Approximately eight months later Janet got a vision from God to head the Entrepreneur Ministry at New Destiny Christian Center, her church home in Florida. She tried to negotiate with God by telling Him she could do a better job of helping the ministry and not leading it, but when God reminded her of the story of Jonah, she surrendered. Janet then fasted and prayed for God's direction as she started to put together the material she would be teaching, and it had become this book. Janet started the first Entrepreneur Class at New Destiny, "How to Start Your Business" in April of 2010 with 40 students. As if that did not keep her busy enough, this young single mom continues to mentor

                                   Olmstead Publishing © 2011

her three sons: De'John, Tevano, and Geovano Green. She often says her first love is God and her second love is her three boys.

Chapter One

The Foundation of a Successful You

Prayer

Introductions

- Your name _____

- Type of business you plan to start

_____

(Take notes from your classmates introductions.)

Group exercise

- Your expectations of the outcomes of this class

(Flip Chart exercise)

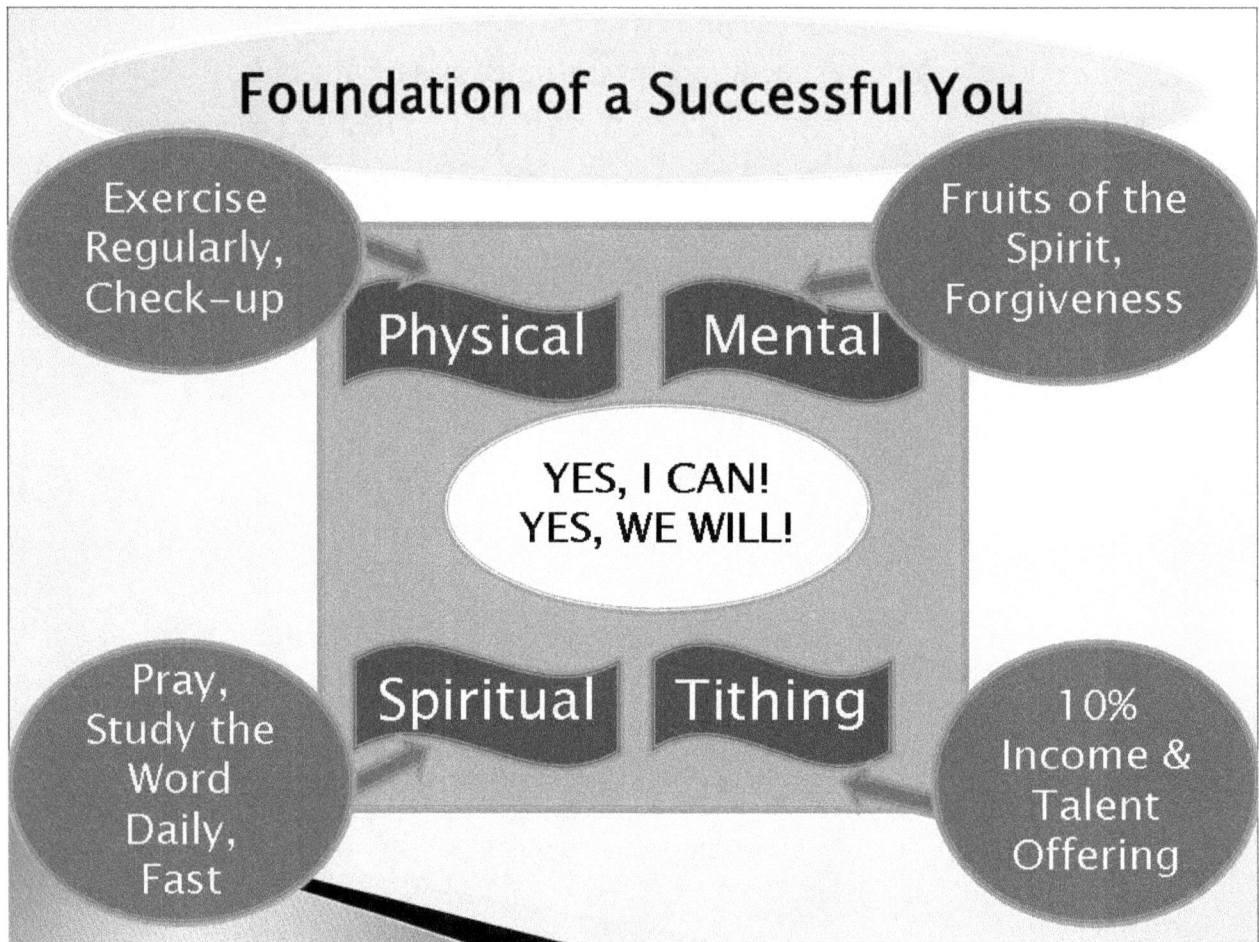

Foundation of a Successful You

Exercise Regularly, Check-up

Fruits of the Spirit, Forgiveness

Physical

Mental

YES, I CAN!
YES, WE WILL!

Pray, Study the Word Daily, Fast

Spiritual

Tithing

10% Income & Talent Offering

Notes:

Scriptural References

◆ Physical   <u>Note your own understanding of each</u>

     ◆ 1ST Corinthians 6:19

     ◆ 2nd Corinthians 6:16

     ◆ 1st Corinthians 3:16

🕊 Spiritual

     🕊 1st Corinthians 7:5

     🕊 2nd Corinthians 11:27

     🕊 Matthew 17:21

🗣   Mental

       🗣 Galatians 5:22-26

       🗣 Matthew 5:44

       🗣 Matthew 6:14

       🗣 James 2:14

       🗣 Romans 12:14-19

💰   Tithing

       💰 Malachi 3:8

       💰 Proverbs 3:9

       💰 Leviticus 27:30

       💰 Matthews 5:23-24

Five keys to Financial Prosperity and Successful Business

1. _____
   _____
   _____
   _____
   _____

2. _____
   _____
   _____
   _____
   _____

3. _____
   _____
   _____
   _____
   _____

4. _____
   _____
   _____
   _____
   _____

5. _____
   _____
   _____
   _____
   _____

Genesis 8:22, King James Version (KJV)

[22]While the earth remaineth, seedtime and harvest, and cold and heat, and summer and winter, and day and night shall not cease.

Extras: Is God giving us instructions? What is your response? Do you act in faith or simply disobey his command? God is **ALWAYS** talking to us. Are we listening to Him? *Allow yourself to be used by God and be obedient to his words. In life when we speak to someone or ask someone a question, we stop talking and listen for their response to our questions. Imagine if we should do the same to God how much better our lives will be. Spend private time with God. Listen to His responses to your questions. Just be still in his presence you will be amazed of what you hear from Him.*

Olmstead Publishing © 2011

Chapter One Assignment

▶ Exercise at least 15 minutes per day for six days per week. Start with a light exercise such as walking. Please consult your Physician before starting any exercise program.

Day	S	M	T	W	Tr	F	Sa
Minutes							

▶ Spend quality time with God each day by praying and reading His Word (increase this time daily).

Day	S	M	T	W	Tr	F	Sa
Minutes							

▶ Start to disconnect from all your negative associations.

▶ Start to develop positive associations.

▶ Fast at least one day this week. Fasting day: _____

  ⋛ Asking God to close all doors that need to be closed and to open doors that need to be opened in your life, according to His will. **Warning …** You must be ready for changes before you pray this prayer (See prayer below).

- Ask God for His guidance and direction for your new business according to His will.

- Pray and ask God to develop your hearing so you can hear His voice clearly.

- Pray and ask God for the knowledge, wisdom, grace, and understanding to start this new venture.

Start sowing seeds with your talent. Sign up to volunteer in a ministry at your church, local hospital or school.

Read Psalm 1 and Psalm 91 daily.

Prayer

Father God I come to you with thanksgiving and praises. I thank You for all You have done in my life and all that You are about to do. I acknowledge You as my Savior, Provider, Healer, Protector, and my All In All. Heavenly Father, I come to You in Jesus Christ's Holy Name. I ask You Lord Jesus Christ according to **John 14:13-14**, (King James Version (KJV)):[13] And whatsoever ye shall ask in my name, that will I do, that the Father may be glorified in the Son. [14] If ye shall ask any thing in my name, I will do it. I ask that You closed all doors that need to be closed in my life and open all doors that need to be opened in my life according to your will for my life, in Jesus' name I pray. Amen.

Thank you, Jesus! Thank you, Lord!

Chapter Two

Personal Development

Please complete the following exercise prior to next class

How I Spend My Time Each 24 Hours					
	TV/ Internet	Family/ Working	Self (exercise)	Prayer, Mediation, The Word	Sleep
Monday					
Tuesday					
Wednesday					
Thursday					
Friday					
Saturday					
Sunday					

Notes:

Grudge Exercise.

List everyone with which you have a grudge.

_____

_____

_____

_____

- Take a few minutes to think about the situation/s.
- Allow yourself to forgive you.
- Ask the individual to forgive you prior to continuing the next chapter in this book.
- Pray for God to give you the grace to release the situation and move on to His greatness for your life.

Select a Prayer Partner

- A prayer partner should believe in the dreams and visions you have for your business. He or she should be spiritually connected to God. You both should pray together at least once a week (choose someone of the same gender). Take a week to pray for someone else. During this week, fast from praying for yourself because your prayer partner should be praying for you. Do you remember the story of Job? God turned his situation around when he prayed for someone else.

- Read Psalm 23rd with your prayer partner and personalize it for each other (insert your prayer partner's name in the blanks).

1 The LORD is _____ **'s** shepherd, _____ **will** lack nothing. [2] He makes _____ lie down in green pastures, he leads _____ beside quiet waters, [3] he refreshes _____ **'s** soul. He guides _____ along the right paths for his name's sake. [4] Even though _____ walk**s** through the darkest valley,[a]_____ will fear no evil, for you are with _____; your rod and your staff, they comfort _____. [5] You prepare a table before _____ in the presence of _____ enemies. You anoint _____ **'s** head with oil; _____ **'s** cup overflows. [6] Surely your goodness and love will follow _____ all the days of _____ **'s** life, and _____ will dwell in the house of the LORD forever. **Amen.**

Ask yourself the following questions. If your responses are yes then you are on the right track.

- Am I starting the right business?

- Can I use my gifts and talents in this business?

- Do I enjoy performing the duties in this business?

- Has God communicated with me regarding this venture?

- Would I perform the activities in this business for free?

- Do I have a passion for this business?

Meet with your immediate family members to communicate your business venture and solicit their help.

Be mindful that this vision is from God to you. Your family members will not have the same level of excitement that you have or the level of understanding for this business venture. Do not be disappointed if they do not embrace your new venture with the same level of excitement you have. Instead, stay positive and express how important it would be to you for them to support your new venture. Allow them to ask questions and answer their questions honestly. Give each family member an assignment according to their gifts, abilities, and personalities. This will allow them to feel as if they are a part of your new venture.

List some of the areas in which family members can help.

1. _____

2. _____

3. _____

4. _____

5. _____

6. _____

7. _____

8. _____

9. _____

10. _____

Details and Notes:

List everyone you speak with more than twice per week

First names of people I speak with on a weekly basis	Topics We Discuss		
	Business Yes No	Building Spirituality Yes No	Other, People Yes No
Total			

Chapter Two Assignment

▸ Exercise at least 20 minutes a day for five days per week.

Day	Sun	Mon	Tues	Wed	Thur	Fri	Sat
Time							

📖 Spend quality time with God each day thanking him for this new venture.

📖 Begin to praise God and thank Him for answering your prayers.

📖 Thank God for choosing you for this business venture.

📖 Lose all your negative associations.

📖 Continue to develop positive associations.

📖 Meet with your immediate family members to communicate your new business venture and solicit their help (pray before and after your meeting). Schedule a meeting time and place that is suitable for everyone involved. Meeting place and time: _____

📖 Fast at least one day this week. Fasting day: _____

🕊 Continue sowing seeds with your talents and offerings.

💰 Give your tithes (10% of all income you receive).

📖 Read Psalm 1 and Psalm 91 daily.

Daily Confirmation

Read at least three per day

Read the following declarations daily, as they will help to strengthen you relationship with God.

<u>Daily Declaration</u>

Matthew 7:7-8, King James Version (KJV)

[7]Ask, and it shall be given you; seek, and ye shall find; knock, and it shall be opened unto you: [8]For every one that asketh receiveth; and he that seeketh findeth; and to him that knocketh it shall be opened.

Proverbs 11:27, King James Version (KJV)

[27]He that diligently seeketh good procureth favour: but he that seeketh mischief, it shall come unto him.

Matthew 17:20, King James Version (KJV)

[20]And Jesus said unto them, Because of your unbelief: for verily I say unto you, If ye have faith as a grain of mustard seed, ye shall say unto this mountain, Remove hence to yonder place; and it shall remove; and nothing shall be impossible unto you.

Luke 6:38, King James Version (KJV)

[38]Give, and it shall be given unto you; good measure, pressed down, and shaken together, and running over, shall men give into your bosom. For with the same measure that ye mete withal it shall be measured to you again.

Olmstead Publishing © 2011

Luke 1:28, King James Version (KJV)

[28]And the angel came in unto her, and said, Hail, thou that art highly favoured, the Lord is with thee: blessed art thou among women.

Deuteronomy 8:18, King James Version (KJV)

[18]But thou shalt remember the LORD thy God: for it is he that giveth thee power to get wealth, that he may establish his covenant which he sware unto thy fathers, as it is this day.

Psalm 112:3, King James Version (KJV)

[3]Wealth and riches shall be in his house: and his righteousness endureth for ever.

2 Corinthians 9:8, King James Version (KJV)

[8]And God is able to make all grace abound toward you; that ye, always having all sufficiency in all things, may abound to every good work:

1 Peter 5:7, King James Version (KJV)

[7]Casting all your care upon him; for he careth for you.

Psalm 1:3, King James Version (KJV)

[3]And he shall be like a tree planted by the rivers of water, that bringeth forth his fruit in his season; his leaf also shall not wither; and whatsoever he doeth shall prosper.

Proverbs 10:22, King James Version (KJV)

²²The blessing of the LORD, it maketh rich, and he addeth no sorrow with it.

Deuteronomy 28:8, King James Version (KJV)

⁸The LORD shall command the blessing upon thee in thy storehouses, and in all that thou settest thine hand unto; and he shall bless thee in the land which the LORD thy God giveth thee.

Psalm 37:4, King James Version (KJV)

⁴Delight thyself also in the LORD: and he shall give thee the desires of thine heart.

Malachi 3:10-11, King James Version (KJV)

¹⁰Bring ye all the tithes into the storehouse, that there may be meat in mine house, and prove me now herewith, saith the LORD of hosts, if I will not open you the windows of heaven, and pour you out a blessing, that there shall not be room enough to receive it.
¹¹And I will rebuke the devourer for your sakes, and he shall not destroy the fruits of your ground; neither shall your vine cast her fruit before the time in the field, saith the LORD of hosts.

Isaiah 54:17, King James Version (KJV)

¹⁷No weapon that is formed against thee shall prosper; and every tongue that shall rise against thee in judgment thou shalt condemn. This is the heritage of the servants of the LORD, and their righteousness is of me, saith the LORD.

3 John 1:2, King James Version (KJV)

[2]Beloved, I wish above all things that thou mayest prosper and be in health, even as thy soul prospereth.

Deuteronomy 28:1, King James Version (KJV)

[1]And it shall come to pass, if thou shalt hearken diligently unto the voice of the LORD thy God, to observe and to do all his commandments which I command thee this day, that the LORD thy God will set thee on high above all nations of the earth

Deuteronomy 28:12, King James Version (KJV)

[12]The LORD shall open unto thee his good treasure, the heaven to give the rain unto thy land in his season, and to bless all the work of thine hand: and thou shalt lend unto many nations, and thou shalt not borrow.

Effective Prayer

- Always start your prayers with thanksgiving. Make your requests known to God (reminder God's will for your life is always better) and end your prayer with, "In Jesus' name, I pray. Amen."

- Ask God to give you the grace to not miss your visitations

- Plant a seed

- Command the devil to remove his hands from your finances, health, and children or whatever you asking of God.

- Claim it

- Dispatch ministering angels to gather your harvest

- Speak yourself into the future or what you believe God for and do not live by your circumstances.

- Begin to believe that God has answered your prayers by praising and thanking Him in advance.

Be patient and wait for God to fulfill your requests according to His will. Be sure to praise God as you wait. Reminder: God's timeframe is not our timeframe.

Olmstead Publishing © 2011

Chapter Three

Business Plan Outline

1. Speak with people, both successful and not successful within your line of business.

2. Filter the information you received. Use that which is applicable to your

3. Allow yourself to record best practices and note reasons for business failure.

4. As you build your business implement the great ideas you have received and do not repeat the ones that causes business failure.

5. Select a Business Mentor, this should be someone that supports your dream and believe in your success. Do not be in a rush to select one. Pray and wait on God's divine connection.

Business Plan

Your Business Plan is the blueprint for your business. Therefore, you should spend quality time working on clearly defining your business model. Use clear and simple language to communicate your ideas, and visions. A well-written business plan will play a key role in the success of your business. You will also need your business plan for loans and certifications.

Sketch Your Business Plan

Company Description

- Mission Statement

- Company Goals and Objectives

- Business Philosophy

- Future Plans

Industry Analysis

- Industry

- Future Trends & Strategic Opportunities

- Company Strengths & Core Competencies

   Olmstead Publishing © 2011

Related Services and Products

- Products

- Services

Target Market Sector

- Three Major Segments

- Customer Profiles

- Competitive Strategy

Marketing Plan & Strategy

- Market Penetration

- Marketing Strategy

- Marketing Plan

- Effort

Operations

- Employee Training & Education

- System & Controls

- Production

- Services

Management & Organization

- Management Structure

  You

- Ownership

- Milestones

- Risk Evaluation

Appendices

Chapter Three Assignment

▶ Exercise at least 25 minutes per day for five days a week.

Day	Sun	Mon	Tues	Wed	Thur	Fri	Sat
Time							

▶ Spend quality time with God each day thanking Him for His direction with your new business.

▶ Start to formulate your business Goals and Objectives for your Business Plan.

▶ Thank God for closing all doors that need to be closed and for opening all doors that need to be opened in your life.

▶ Embrace your new positive associations.

▶ Thank God in advance for developing your hearing so you can hear Him speaking to you clearly.

🕊 Continue sowing seeds with your talents and offerings.

💰 Pay your tithes (10% of all income you receive).

📖 Read Psalm 1 and Psalm 91 daily.

Chapter Four

Forming Your Business
Determine the Legal Structure of Your Business

For this subject matter of determining your business structure, I totally recommend that you consult an Accountant. It is important that you consider your tax saving options for your unique business. Below are the different types of legal structures one should consider when starting their business.

▶ **Sole Proprietorship -**

_____

_____

▶ **Partnership -**

_____

_____

▶ **Corporation -**

_____

_____

▶ **S Corporation -**

_____

_____

_____

▶ **Limited Liability Company (LLC) -**

_____

_____

_____

▶ **Non Profit -**

_____

_____

_____

▶ **Cooperative -**

_____

_____

Chapter Four Assignment

▶ Exercise at least 30 minutes per day for three days per week.

Day	Sun	Mon	Tues	Wed	Thur	Fri	Sat
Time							

▶ Spend quality time with God each day thanking Him for His direction with your new business.

▶ Thank God for closing all doors that need to be closed and for opening doors that need to be opened in your life.

▶ Ask God for His grace through the transition and ask Him to provide a prayer partner and a mentor according to His will.

▶ Continue to embrace your new positive associations.

▶ Continue to formulate your Business Plan.

▶ Discuss and brainstorm your business name with your family members and mentor(s).

▶ Thank God for developing your hearing so you can hear His voice clearly.

🕊 Continue sowing seeds with your talents and offerings.

💰 Pay your tithes (10% of all income you receive).

📖 Read Psalm 1 and Psalm 91 daily.

How to Choose Your Business Location

Location is a Key Element to the Success of Your Business

What are some questions you should ask yourself when choosing a business location?

1. _____

2. _____

3. _____

4. _____

5. _____

6. _____

7. _____

8. _____

9. _____

 Olmstead Publishing © 2011

Chapter Five Assignment

▸ Exercise at least 35 minutes per day for five days per week.

Day	Sun	Mon	Tues	Wed	Thur	Fri	Sat
Time							

▸ Spend quality time with God each day thanking Him for His direction with your new business.

▸ Thank God for closing all doors that need to be closed and for opening doors that need to be opened in your life.

▸ Thank God for His grace through this transition period.

▸ Continue to embrace your new positive associations.

▸ Continue to formulate your business plan. Start to research your local SCORE office and make contact with the Small Business Administration office, which will assist you with your business plan.

▸ Discuss and brainstorm your business name with your family members and mentor(s).

▸ Thank God for developing your hearing so you can hear His voice clearly. Spend quiet time with God daily.

🕊 Continue sowing seeds with your talents and offerings.

💰 Pay your tithes (10% of all income you receive).

📖 Read Psalm 1 and Psalm 91 daily.

Olmstead Publishing © 2011

Chapter Six

Positioning Your Business for Success

Advertizing and Marketing Your Business

ⓘ Congratulations you are on your way to becoming a new business owner.

Once you have completed the required document by law, now it is time to proceed with marketing your business.

1. Create business cards and flyers with easy to read fonts and list five things you should have on your business card.

     a. _____

     b. _____

     c. _____

     d. _____

     e. _____

Sample Business Card

Sketch a Business Card for Yourself

List below the items, in addition to those on your business card that you would want to put on the flyer. Sketch out a flyer in the block below using those components.

List here:

2. List here people who should know about your business, then tell everyone that will listen to you about your business. They might not be able to use your services now, but they can refer you to someone that will.

3. Place an advertisement in your local newspaper's business section. This is sometimes free. Try writing the advertisement here.

4. Send flyers out to businesses/residents within a thirty-mile radius of your business. Speak with your local post office representative or print shop and they will assist you.

5. Find large shopping centers within a five-mile radius of your business and place flyers on vehicles or distribute flyers to people leaving the major department stores. You should be able to pay a reliable high school student to do this. Make sure you are not breaking the respective city laws with any of your guerilla marketing efforts.

6. Speak with local school administrators and your church representatives about placing an ad in their bulletin.

7. Attend at least two networking events per week and start to promote your business.

Day	Sun	Mon	Tues	Wed	Thurs	Fri	Sat
Time							
Event							

Olmstead Publishing © 2011

8. Sponsor a charitable event. Make sure the ROI (Return on Investment) is worth it. Measure the number of attendees and make them among your targeted customers. Plan and describe below.

9. Join professional organizations that support your specific type of business.

10. Internet search and research all free local advertising agencies.

Ask your bank if you may set up a table in the lobby to promote your **New Business** at least twice a month for three months. Your bank would definitely love to see your business flourish, so get their input on how they can help you advertise.

Social Media

1. Pay a professional to create a website that represents your company image. Research other websites within your line of business. This will give you a better idea of how you want yours to look.

2. Create a Facebook® account. If you are not sure how to use Facebook®, give this project to your young teenage or young adult children, nieces, nephews, or cousins.

3. Creating a Twitter® account is another fabulous idea. Make sure you will have the time to blog and keep up with the communications required. Remember, this is a reflection on your business so you need to maintain the image you are trying to portray.

Name some additional social media you can use to promote your business?

1. _____

2. _____

3. _____

4. _____

5. _____

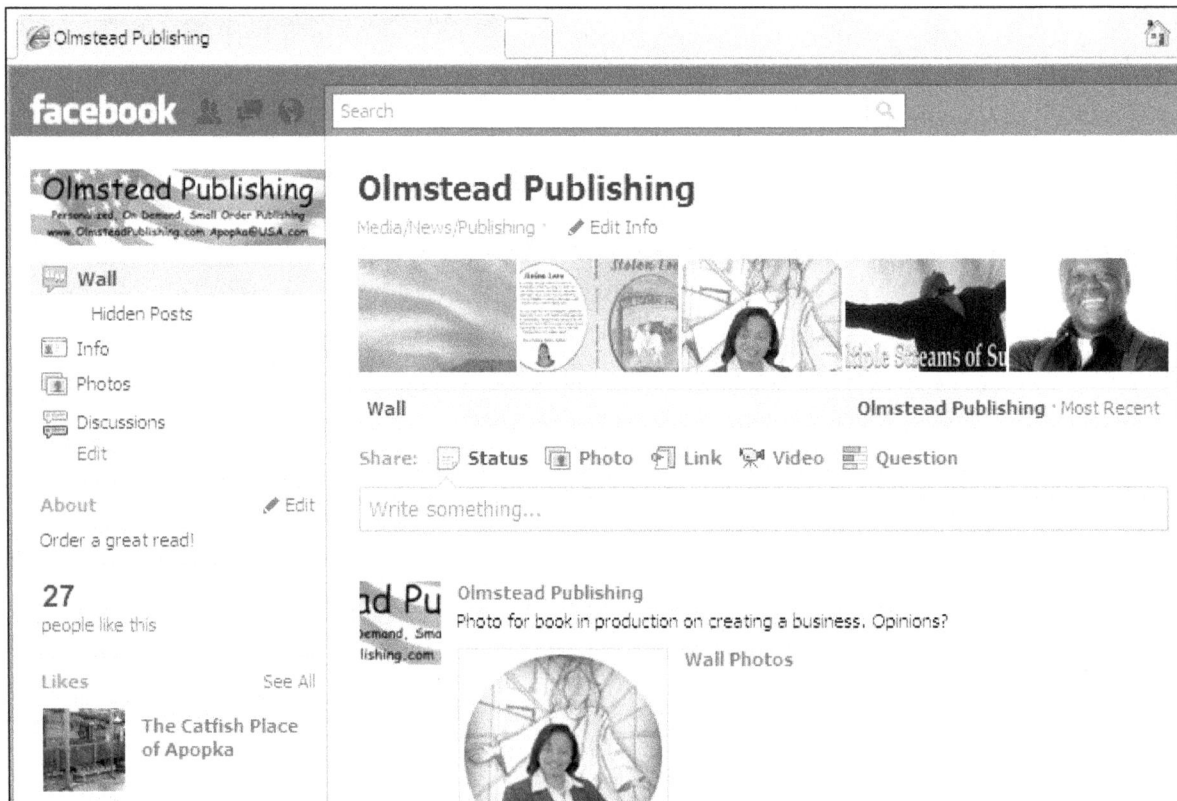

Chapter Six Assignment

▸ Exercise at least 40 minutes per day for five days per week.

Day	Sun	Mon	Tues	Wed	Thur	Fri	Sat
Time							

▸ Spend quality time with God each day thanking Him for His direction with your new business.

▸ Thank God for closing all doors that need to be closed and for opening doors that need to be opened in your life.

▸ Thank God for His grace through this transition period.

▸ Thank God for your new positive associations.

▸ Thank God for giving you the desire to have a prayer partner and mentor in your life.

▸ Thank God for developing your hearing so you can hear His voice clearly and spend quiet time with Him daily.

🕊 Continue sowing seeds with your talents and offerings. Remember, you cannot out-give God).

💰 Pay your tithes (10% of all income you receive).

📖 Read Psalm 1 and Psalm 91 daily.

Chapter Seven

Selecting a Successful Team

Congratulations, your business is flourishing and now you need to hire some good help. Listed below are some guidelines to follow so you can reduce staffing costs and at the same time maintain a productive staff.

Making the Right Hiring Decision

What are some things to consider when hiring your staff?

1. _____

2. _____

3. _____

4. _____

5. _____

6. _____

Now you are ready to proceed with interviews

○ Schedule quality time (at least 1 hour of uninterrupted time) to interview each candidate.

○ Create an application for your use.

    ▶ There are free employment applications online. Verify with your local Department of Labor or Workforce Office for state and federal requirements.

    ▶ Employment applications should include an "at will" clause that states either party can terminate the employment contract or agreement at will and with no liability.

○ Have all applicants complete an employment application.

    ▶ Have at least one other person you trust to independently interview the candidate. If it is a management position, use at least three interviewers.

    ▶ Record answers to your questions during your interviews.

    ▶ Have no distractions during interviews (i.e., phone calls.)

    ▶ Ask open-ended questions. (Questions that **do not** require a yes or no answer)

Making the Right Hiring Decision

- Listen for previous employment behavior and think of it as a future behavior.

- Pay attention to body language. The candidate should be able to look you in the eyes when responding to your questions. If he or she fails to do so chances are the candidate is not telling the truth, or is possibly hiding something. Yet, be aware that some cultures do not look superiors in the eye out of respect. Do disregard them in these instances.

- Listen for team player clues.

- Contemplate the choice of deciding between the most **qualified** person versus the most **suitable** person for a position. Are you willing to hire someone that has all the required credentials and no work history, versus someone who has the proven work history and no credentials?

- Adhere to established hiring practices and be consistent with all applicants. Do not show favoritism.

- Always check references and check a minimum of three references.

Olmstead Publishing © 2011

- Consistency with employees minimizes discrimination lawsuits. If you conduct background checks and require drug testing, do the same for all employees. Check with your state for up to date labor laws.

- Have an established wage scale and be consistent with all employees.

List ten things you should do to maintain a successful work force.

1. _____

2. _____

3. _____

4. _____

5. _____

6. _____

7. _____

8. _____

9. _____

10. _____

What are your employer responsibilities to your employees?

1. _____

2. _____

3. _____

4. _____

5. _____

6. _____

7. _____

8. _____

9. _____

10. _____

11. _____

Chapter Seven Assignment

▶ Exercise at least 45 minutes per day for four days per week.

Day	Sun	Mon	Tues	Wed	Thur	Fri	Sat
Time							

▶ Spend quality time with God each day thanking Him for His direction with your new business.

▶ Thank God for closing all doors that need to be closed and for opening doors that need to be opened in your life.

▶ Thank God for His grace through this transition period.

▶ Thank God for your new positive associations.

▶ Thank God for giving you the desire to have a prayer partner and mentor in your life.

▶ Continue to formulate your Business Plan.

▶ Research local Chambers of Commerce and schedule your first Networking Event. At this point, you are attending only to observe. Explain selection here:

▸ Research the company name you have chosen on your local Business Administration website. Recommendation: Seek an Accountant's assistance when registering your business name. Make notes here:

▸ Thank God for developing your hearing so you can hear His voice clearly.

𝕐 Continue sowing seeds with your talents and offerings.

💰 Pay your tithes (10% of all earnings you receive).

📖 Read Psalm 1 and Psalm 91 daily.

Chapter Eight

Your Business Start-up Expense (Accounting)

Complete the following information below which will give you a true picture of what you need to start your business. Some areas may not apply to your respective business.

Startup Expenses—Company Name:

Basis of Capital

Owners' Investment (Name and percent of ownership)

Your name   Percent of Ownership

Other investor

Other investor

Total Investment _____

Bank Loans

Bank 1

Bank 2

Total Bank Loans_____

Other Loans

Sources

Total Other Loans_____

Startup Expenses

Real Estate/Building

Construction

Purchases

Remodeling

Other

Total _____

Leasehold Improvements

Item 1

Item 2

Item 3

Item 4

Total _____

Capital Equipment List

Furniture

Equipment

Fixtures

Machinery

Other

Total _____

Location and Administrative Expenses

Rental Equipment

Utility deposits

Legal and accounting fees

Prepaid insurance

Pre-opening salaries

Other

Total _____

Opening Inventory

Stage 1

Stage 2

Stage 3

Stage 4

Stage 5

Total Inventory _____

Notes:

Advertising and Marketing Expenses

Advertising

Signage

Printing

Other/additional signage

Total _____

Other Expenses

Other expense

Other expense

Total _____

Notes:

Working Capital

Summary Statement

Sources of Capital

Owner's and other investments

Bank loans

Other loans

Total Source of Funds _____

Startup Expenses

Buildings/real estate

Leasehold improvements

Capital equipment

Location/administration expenses

Opening inventory

Advertising/Marketing expenses

Other expenses

Working capital

Total Startup Expenses _____

Notes:

Security for Loan Proposal

Security for Loans	Value	Description
Real estate		
Other Security		
Other Security		
Other Security		

Owners

Your name

Other owner

Other owner

Other owner

Other Loan Guarantors

Loan guarantor 1

Loan guarantor 2

Loan guarantor 3

Notes:

Chapter Eight Assignment

▶ Exercise at least 45 minutes per day for four days per week.

Day	Sun	Mon	Tues	Wed	Thur	Fri	Sat
Time							

▶ Spend quality time with God each day thanking Him for His direction with your new business.

    ▶ Thank God for His grace through this transition period.

▶ Select a mentor and a prayer partner. Do not be in a rush to do so if your spirit does not lead you.

▶ Attend a networking event (at this point, you should already be promoting your business).

Event	Date	Time	Place

▶ Continue to formulate your Business Plan.

▸ Congratulations, you have now selected a company name for your business.

Name: _____

▸ Research all the companies in your city that promote businesses free.

▶ Thank God for developing your hearing so you can hear His voice clearly. Spend quiet time with God daily.

🕊 Continue sowing seeds with your talents and offerings.

💰 Pay your tithes (10% of all earnings you receive).

📖 Read Psalm 1 and Psalm 91 daily.

Chapter Nine

Growing Your Business

Successful Networking

In order to build a successful business you need a great customer/client base. Since your business is new and you are trying to build your customer base, I would recommend that you attend at least one networking event per week. Be more concerned about building a business relationship rather than just handing out business cards. Remember, a recommendation is always better than a referral. It is also a good idea to volunteer your time with charitable organizations because in order to reap a harvest you have to sow seeds first.

List ten things you should do in preparation

for a successful networking event

1. _____

2. _____

3. _____

4. _____

5. _____

6. _____

7. _____

8. _____

9. _____

10._____

Reminder: The best way to sell your business is not to sell it. Build a business relationship first, because a recommendation is always better than a referral.

Class Networking Exercise:

How I Spend My Time Each 24 Hours					
	TV/ Internet	Family/ Working	Self/ Exercising	God/ Prayer/ The Word	Sleeping
Monday					
Tuesday					
Wednesday					
Thursday					
Friday					
Saturday					
Sunday					

Olmstead Publishing © 2011

Chapter Nine Assignment

▶ Exercise at least one hour per day for four days per week.

Day	Sun	Mon	Tues	Wed	Thur	Fri	Sat
Time							

▶ Spend quality time with God each day thanking Him for His divine favor and divine connections for your new business.

▶ Thank God for His grace through this transition period.

▶ Select a mentor and a prayer partner. If you are not comfortable with anyone you know continue to praise God for one anyway. Do not rush this process.

▶ Attend at least two networking events per month. Always pray for divine connections and favor from God before you attend these events.

Event	Date	Time	Location

▶ Continue to formulate your Business Plan. Have a professional a representative from your local Score or SBA (Small Business Administration) office to review your Business Plan.

▶ Think about members in your family, church, and community that you might be able to employ in your business. Pray to God for guidance through this process.

✍ Research all the companies in your city that promote businesses for free and promote your business with the reputable companies.

▶ Thank God for speaking to you and submit yourself to His will.

🕊 Continue sowing seeds with your talents and offerings.

💰 Pay your tithes (10% of all income you receive).

📖 Read Psalm 1 and Psalm 91 daily.

Chapter 10

Stay Encouraged

List twenty things you have learned in this class:

1. _____

2. _____

3. _____

4. _____

5. _____

6. _____

7. _____

8. _____

9. _____

10. _____

11._____

12._____

13._____

14._____

15._____

16._____

17._____

18._____

19._____

20._____

Reminders

✝ You **must** have a personal relationship with God

    ✝ Pray

    ✝ Fast

    ✝ Meditate on God's words

    ✝ Spend quiet uninterrupted time with yourself

    ✝ Spend quiet uninterrupted time with God

        o Pray each day and ask God for your assignment that day and that you will not miss any of his visitations

🕊 Sow seeds

    🕊 Your time

    🕊 Your finances

    🕊 Your talent

    🕊 Introduce this ministry to at least two people who needs to start their business

    🕊 As you climb the ladder of success be a mentor to someone else (Pass the torch)

⚫ Stay faithful

⚫ As you wait for your business breakthrough, volunteer your time at a charitable organization

⚫ Have a Prayer Warrior Team (PWT) for yourself. Your PWT is at least two people you can call anytime for prayer, to fast, and intercede with you. These people should be more like your spiritual confidants. You should be able to share your unedited feelings with them.

🗣 Build your networking group

🗣 Get involved with local chambers and charitable organization

🗣 Allow yourself to be in the presence of positive people and business owner

🗣 Attend at least two networking event per week

👪 Stay connected with your mentor, myself, your prayer partner and prayer warrior

👪 Create a monthly support group for Kingdom Business Owners

List some positive friends and colleagues that you may invite.

I believe the process of starting your business is like a pregnant woman. During the first trimester, the pregnant woman goes through the phase of what we call "morning sickness." She is nauseous, yet excited. Aspiring business owners, during their first couple of months, become very anxious and nervous all at once. Sometimes asking themselves, "Am I doing the right thing?" Both the pregnant woman and the aspiring business owners continue to plan for that big day that they will give birth. Business owners will give birth to a new business while the pregnant woman will give birth to a child. Both will go through the exciting stage of buying clothes for her newborn, the other selecting the business name and of sharing the idea of opening a new business. Both types of parents are excited and happy.

As the birthing stage draws near, both the pregnant woman and the aspiring business owners, start to feel tension. For both, the tension stems from something within them that wants to give birth or come forth. The pregnant woman can touch her stomach and feel the baby inside of her. She talks to it and comforts it. The aspiring business owners have God to speak with confirming that he or she knows that God will help them to birth their new ideas. This is where faith can separate the two. The pregnant woman has not seen what is inside of her but she trust her doctor that it is a baby. Therefore, she treats her pregnancy as if she is carrying a human being in her womb. How much more should we trust God that with whatever he has impregnated us, we will also give birth?

Every so often, when a pregnant woman goes into labor, she pushes her way through the pain. The first stage the pain might be thirty minutes apart. Because she had prepared herself for this moment, she knows what breathing technique to use to relief her pain. As the pains get closer together, she pushes harder and longer. At no point does she quit. She knows something is inside of her needs to be birthed. As she pushes through the pain, with her mother on the left and her husband on the right, she knows no one else can do the work. The tougher the pain the harder she knows she has to push.

On the other hand, you have aspiring business owners who start to feel challenged that might be from an issue of getting all the required permits approved for a new building, or not being able to get approved for the equipment loan, or just not being able to find the perfect location for the business. The aspiring business owners become weary and start to question their selves, "Am I doing the right thing?" This is where many aspiring business owners fail or quit. They do not push themselves through the challenges, as a woman in labor would. They just throw in the towel or let their dreams fade away. Don't you know it is the plan of the devil to put up roadblocks just as you are about to cross the finish line? Just as you reach one level that would then transcend into another level. Just as a woman in labor would push her way through the pain, so should you. The stronger the pain the harder you should Push! Push! Push! Moreover, if you feel you cannot push anymore, **bring out all your weapons, its wartime and God is with you so you will conquer in Jesus' name.**

1. The Bible has a verse for all situations. Speak God's words over your situation. **"No weapons formed against me shall prosper," "Through God all things are possible," "I am the lender and not the barrower," "I live by faith, and not by sight," "By Your favor, Lord, You have established me a strong mountain."** Speak God's words until they come alive.

2. Call your prayer warrior and unite in prayer and fasting.

3. Never give up on God's will for your life.

Your challenges build your experience pool that turns you into an expert in your field. So embrace your setbacks and consider them as your downtime for better preparation. Use them as your steps to another level of greatness. When you have done everything, you are supposed to do, **be still and trust God**. His timing is not our timing. He is always on time. God is never late. Always believe His words. He never lies. His words are final. You will be successful if you trust God.

Summary To Do List

_____

_____

_____

_____

_____

_____

_____

_____

_____

_____

_____

_____

_____

_____

_____

_____

_____

Thanks to the Following

Dr. Zachery Tims
New Destiny Christian Center
505 East McCormick Ave
Apopka, Florida 32707
407-884-6322

New Destiny Christian Center Entrepreneur Minister
505 East McCormick Ave
Apopka, Florida 32707
407-884-6322
destinybusiness@ndcc.tv

Ms Sonia Troupe
Fromtheheart Photography
Troupetrouper@AOL.com
407-470-9072

PUBLISHER
Olmstead Publishing
www.OlmsteadPublishing.com
Apopka@usa.com

Book Contact
Janet Green
PO Box 691966
Orlando Fl 32869
407-925-1652
www.janetbusiness.com
howto@janetbusiness.com

When Emailing:
Please include a testimony of any insights
you have received from this book.

www.ingramcontent.com/pod-product-compliance
Lightning Source LLC
Chambersburg PA
CBHW062108090426
42741CB00015B/3359